When Butterflies Cross the Sky

THE MONARCH BUTTERFLY MIGRATION

by Sharon Katz Cooper

illustrated by Joshua S. Brunet

PICTURE WINDOW BOOKS

a capstone imprint

Thanks to our advisers for their expertise, research, and advice:

Wendy Caldwell, Program Coordinator, Monarch Joint Venture
University of Minnesota, Twin Cities

Terry Flaherty, PhD, Professor of English
Minnesota State University, Mankato

Editor: Jill Kalz
Designer: Lori Bye
Art Director: Nathan Gassman
Production Specialist: Morgan Walters
The illustrations in this book were created with oils,
acrylics, and prisma color pencil.
Image Credit: Shutterstock: ekler, 3 (map)

Picture Window Books are published by Capstone,
1710 Roe Crest Drive, North Mankato, Minnesota 56003
www.capstonepub.com

Library of Congress Cataloging-in-Publication Data
Katz Cooper, Sharon, author.
  When butterflies cross the sky : the monarch butterfly migration / by
Sharon Katz Cooper ; illustrated by Joshua S. Brunet.
     pages cm. — (Nonfiction picture books. Extraordinary migrations)
  Summary: "Follows a single monarch butterfly on its annual migration
journey"—Provided by publisher.
  Audience: K to grade 3.
  Includes bibliographical references and index.
  ISBN 978-1-4795-6076-9 (library binding)
  ISBN 978-1-4795-6104-9 (paper over board)
  ISBN 978-1-4795-6108-7 (eBook PDF)
1. Monarch butterfly—Migration—Juvenile literature. 2. Animal
migration—Juvenile literature. I. Brunet, Joshua S., illustrator. II. Title.
  QL561.D3K38 2015
  595.78'9—dc23   2014024412

EDITOR'S NOTE: There are typically four generations of monarch butterflies in a 12-month period. The first three generations live two to six weeks each. But the fourth generation is special. It lives up to nine months. It is the generation that migrates south in fall. This book tells the story of one fourth-generation monarch butterfly from the northeastern United States.

Printed in the United States of America in North Mankato Minnesota.
102014   008482CGS15

Monarch butterflies weigh less than a dollar bill. Yet every year they migrate up to 2,500 miles (4,023 kilometers) from the United States and southern Canada. Butterflies west of the Rocky Mountains fly to the coast of California. Butterflies east of the Rocky Mountains fly to Mexico. No other butterfly travels so far. Flying about 30 miles (48 km) per day, monarch butterflies make the trip to Mexico in about two months. Why is this journey so important to them?

Flutter, flutter! Flutter, flutter! The butterfly flits from flower to flower. The sun is warm on her wings. She sips nectar with her strawlike tongue and fills herself up. The sweet food will give her energy for the long flight ahead.

Fall arrives. The days grow shorter. A cool breeze swishes the leaves.

The butterfly knows it's time to head south. She cannot survive the long months of freezing weather here. She needs a warmer winter home. So do the other monarchs.

The butterfly joins hundreds of other monarchs in the sky. Air currents lift her, so she doesn't have to beat her wings all the time. She saves energy by gliding.

The butterfly will stop to drink nectar and to rest. But she cannot rest long. She's racing the cold. Even though she's never made this journey before, her body knows the way.

The butterfly's journey is dangerous. She may not find enough food to eat. She may become too tired to finish the trip. Birds and other animals may try to eat her. Bad weather may slow or stop her. She cannot fly in the rain, and she cannot fly if it gets too cold.

Finally, about two months later, the butterfly reaches her winter home. The mountains of central Mexico are perfect for her. The air is cold but not quite freezing. The butterfly can rest and save her energy throughout the winter.

The butterfly settles onto a tree.
Millions of other butterflies do the
same. Blankets of orange and black
butterflies cover the trees.

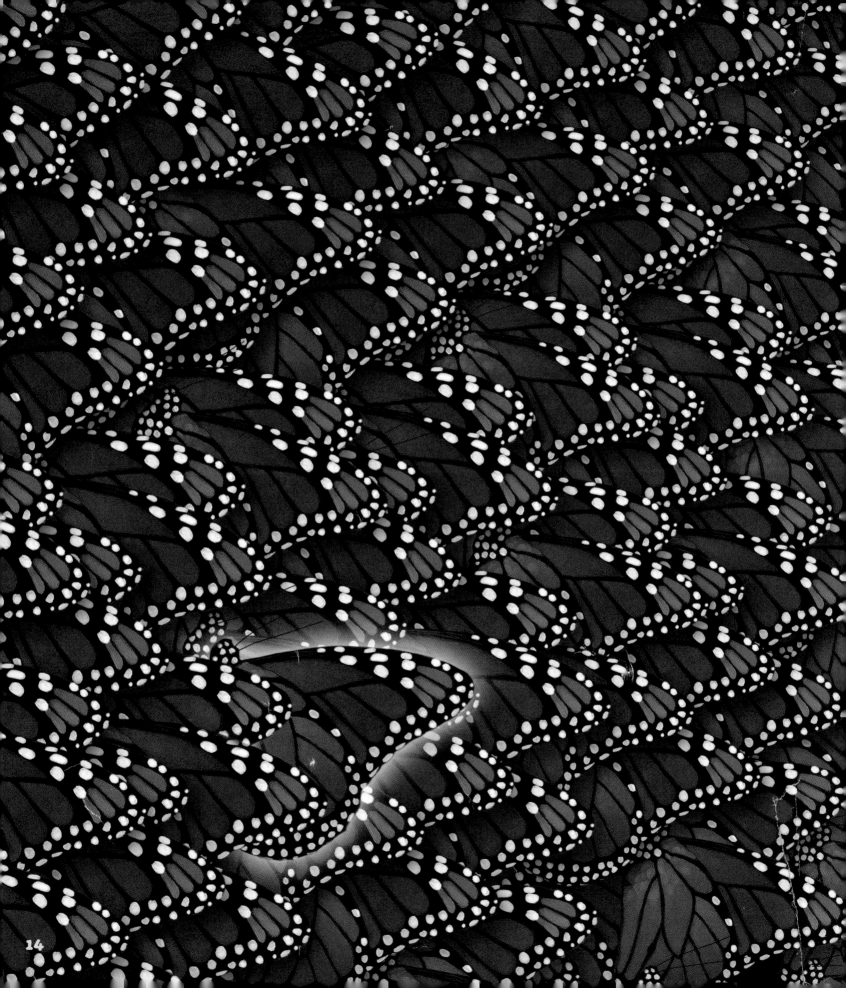

The butterfly is safe for now. She spends the winter resting, clinging to the trees. The trees protect her from predators and bad weather. She drinks water once in a while, but she does not eat much. She stored lots of energy on her journey south.

In late February the butterfly mates. Then it's time to find a place to lay her eggs. There is no milkweed in the mountains of Mexico. The butterfly needs milkweed. It's the only plant on which she will lay her eggs.

The butterfly knows she has to fly north again. Her journey isn't quite over. She has one last job to do.

18

The butterfly leaves Mexico with millions of other monarchs. She lays her eggs on milkweed plants as she heads north. Once her eggs are laid, her long journey ends, and she dies.

After a few days, a tiny, hungry caterpillar hatches from each egg.

The caterpillars eat lots of milkweed. In about two weeks, they're old enough to start changing into adults. They shed their skin and harden into a bright green chrysalis. Great changes happen inside.

About 10 days later, new butterflies crawl out.
They will soon fly away in search of food, a mate,
and the warm summer sun.

Monarch Butterfly Fast Facts

Scientific name: *Danaus plexippus*

Adult weight (average): about 0.02 ounces (0.6 grams)

Adult size: 3.9 inches (10 centimeters) wide

Diet of butterflies: nectar, sipped through a strawlike tongue called a proboscis

Diet of caterpillars: milkweed

Identifying spot: males have a small dark spot on the inside part of their rear wings; females don't

Number of eggs: females lay about 700 eggs

Size of eggs: the size of a pinhead

Lifespan of migratory monarchs: 7 to 9 months

Length of migration: up to 2,500 miles (4,023 kilometers)

Critical Thinking Using the Common Core

1. Why is it important for monarch butterflies to migrate each fall? (Key Ideas and Details)

2. Describe the dangers monarch butterflies face on their migration journey. (Key Ideas and Details)

3. Explain what the map on page 3 is showing. (Craft and Structure)

Glossary

caterpillar—a larva that changes into a butterfly or moth; a caterpillar is the second life stage of a butterfly

chrysalis—the third stage of a butterfly; "pupa" is another word for chrysalis

current—the movement of air in a certain direction

mate—to join together to produce young; a mate is also the male or female partner of a pair of animals

milkweed—a plant with milky juice and pointed pods; monarch butterflies lay eggs only on milkweed

nectar—a sweet liquid found in many flowers

predator—an animal that hunts other animals for food

proboscis—a long tube-shaped mouthpart

shed—to drop or let go of

survive—to stay alive

Read More

Edwards, Roberta. *Flight of the Butterflies.* All Aboard Reader. Station Stop 2. New York: Grosset & Dunlap, 2010.

Marsh, Laura. *Butterflies.* National Geographic Kids. Science Readers. Washington, D.C.: National Geographic; Enfield: Publishers Group UK [distributor], 2010.

Pasternak, Carol. *How to Raise Monarch Butterflies: A Step-by-Step Guide for Kids.* Richmond Hill, Ont.; Buffalo, N.Y.: Firefly Books, 2012.

Waxman, Laura Hamilton. *Let's Look at Monarch Butterflies.* Animal Close-ups. Minneapolis: Lerner Publications, 2011.

Internet Sites

FactHound offers a safe, fun way to find Internet sites related to this book. All of the sites on FactHound have been researched by our staff.

Here's all you do:

Visit www.facthound.com

Type in this code: 9781479560769

Super-cool stuff!

Check out projects, games and lots more at
www.capstonekids.com

Index

LOOK FOR ALL THE BOOKS IN THE SERIES:

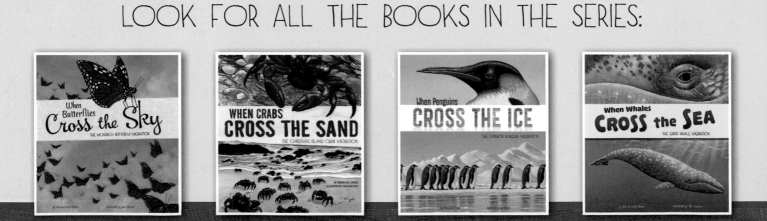

24